FOCUS ON

VIKINGS

ANITA GANERI

GLOUCESTER PRESS
London · New York · Toronto · Sydney

© Aladdin Books Ltd 1992

Designed and produced by
Aladdin Books Ltd
28 Percy Street
London W1P 9FF

First published in
Great Britain in 1992 by
Franklin Watts Ltd
96 Leonard Street
London EC2A 4RH

ISBN 0 7496 1018 2

A CIP catalogue record for this book is
available from the British Library.

Printed in Belgium

Design	David West Children's Book Design
Designer	Flick Killerby
Series Director	Bibby Whittaker
Editors	Fiona Robertson Elise Bradbury
Picture Research	Emma Krikler
Illustrators	Peter Kesteven Dave Burroughs

The author, Anita Ganeri (MA Cantab),
has written many books for children on
history, natural history and other topics.

The educational and historical consultant, Dr
Anne Millard, works for the extra-mural
department of London University. She has
written numerous books for children on
history and archaeology.

INTRODUCTION

The Vikings were sea-faring people from Scandinavia who rose to prominence in northern Europe between the 8th and 11th centuries. Throughout history, the Vikings have been portrayed as fierce, brutal warriors who struck terror and fear into the hearts of the European people. Yet the Vikings have also left an indelible mark on history as brave adventurers, shrewd traders and successful colonists. This book provides the historical background to the Vikings, while linking them with literature, science and maths projects, geographical facts and arts activities. The key below shows how the subjects are divided up. We hope the activities on the following pages will help you to discover the world of the Vikings.

Geography
The symbol of the planet Earth shows where geographical facts and activities are included. These sections look at some of the routes taken by the Viking explorers, and at the lands in which they settled.

Language and literature
An open book is the sign for activities which involve language. These sections explore how everyday words have been influenced by the Vikings. Activities include using the Runic alphabet to write a secret message and describing what it would be like on a Viking raid.

Science

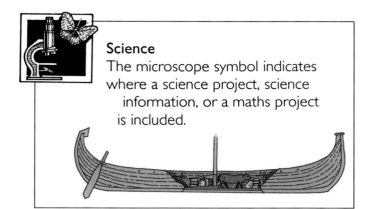

The microscope symbol indicates where a science project, science information, or a maths project is included.

History

The sign of the scroll and hourglass shows where historical information is given. These sections look at key figures and events during the Viking period and examine the impact of Viking society on our society today.

Social history

The symbol of a family shows where information about social history is given.

These sections aim to provide an insight into the everyday lives of the Vikings. Topics covered include what they wore and what kinds of food they ate.

Arts, crafts and music

The symbol showing a sheet of music and art tools signals arts, crafts or musical activities. There are many imaginative ways of recreating Viking artefacts. Projects include making some Viking jewellery and creating natural dyes.

CONTENTS

WHO WERE THE VIKINGS?

The Viking Age lasted from the end of the 8th century AD until the end of the 11th century AD. The Vikings, or Norsemen, came from Scandinavia, from the present-day countries of Denmark, Sweden and Norway. The Vikings are most famous as fierce warriors who looted and conquered many parts of Europe in a series of terrifying raids. However, they were also successful and adventurous traders and explorers, talented poets and skilled shipbuilders and craftsmen.

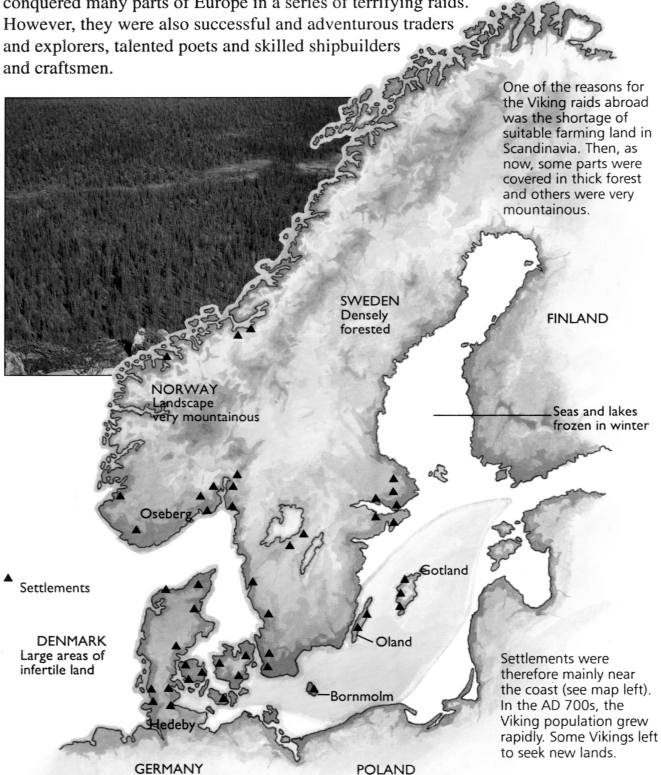

One of the reasons for the Viking raids abroad was the shortage of suitable farming land in Scandinavia. Then, as now, some parts were covered in thick forest and others were very mountainous.

SWEDEN
Densely forested

FINLAND

NORWAY
Landscape very mountainous

Seas and lakes frozen in winter

Oseberg

▲ Settlements

Gotland

DENMARK
Large areas of infertile land

Oland

Bornmolm

Hedeby

Settlements were therefore mainly near the coast (see map left). In the AD 700s, the Viking population grew rapidly. Some Vikings left to seek new lands.

GERMANY   POLAND

4

Classes of society

Viking society was divided into different classes, based on wealth and land ownership. A king, or chief, ruled over each community. Below him came the rich noblemen, or jarls. The English word "earl" comes from the word "jarl". The kings and jarls were the most powerful landowners. Below them came the freemen, or karls. They included farmers, merchants and craftsmen. At the bottom of the ladder were the slaves, who were known as thralls.

JARLS	KARLS	THRALLS
Noblemen	Freemen	Slaves

The Viking name

The Scandinavians did not call themselves Vikings. This was a name used by early writers. The word "Viking" may come from the old Icelandic word "vik", meaning bay or creek. The phrase "a-Viking" also means to go exploring.

The first raid

"...never before has such terror appeared in Britain as we have now suffered from this pagan race..."
This account by the Northumbrian priest, Alcuin, marks the beginning of the Viking reign of terror after their attack on the Holy Island of Lindisfarne in June, AD 793. The Vikings looted the monastery there, killed some of the monks and carried others off to be slaves. The attack on Lindisfarne was terrifying because it was a holy place, known and respected throughout Europe. Also, like other monasteries around the coast of Britain, Lindisfarne had believed itself to be immune to attacks from the sea.

The original monastery at Lindisfarne was completely destroyed by the Vikings. It was later rebuilt (below).

Vikings at work

The majority of Vikings spent quite short periods away from home on raids. They worked as farmers, growing oats, barley, rye and vegetables, and tending cattle, pigs, sheep and goats. Fruits, such as apples, and hazelnuts and walnuts were also grown and stored for use during the winter. Reindeer, rabbit, hare and wild bears were hunted by the Vikings, and cod, salmon and trout were plentiful in the Scandinavian fjords and rivers. Other Vikings were merchants, travelling far and wide to trade their goods (see pages 12-13). Some were specialist craftsmen – silversmiths, blacksmiths and woodcarvers. Most famous of all were the skills of the Viking shipbuilders and sailors (see pages 8-9).

HOME LIFE

Family life was very important to the Vikings. The man was the head of the household, but women were much more independent than elsewhere in Europe. Most Viking houses had only one room in which the whole family cooked, ate and slept. There was very little furniture, and the family's belongings were hung around the walls or stored in benches around the edge of the room. Most of the cooking was done over a fire pit in the centre of the house. There were no windows and only one small hole to let the smoke out, so the houses were often dark and smelly inside.

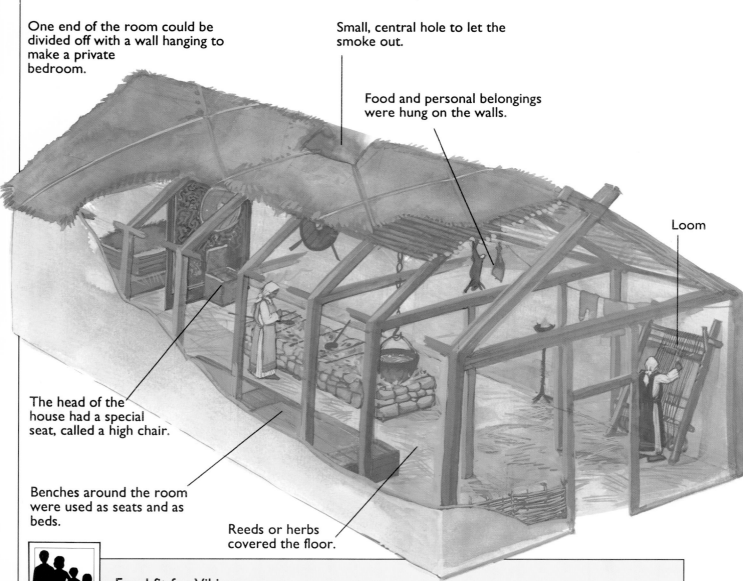

One end of the room could be divided off with a wall hanging to make a private bedroom.

Small, central hole to let the smoke out.

Food and personal belongings were hung on the walls.

Loom

The head of the house had a special seat, called a high chair.

Benches around the room were used as seats and as beds.

Reeds or herbs covered the floor.

Food fit for Vikings

The Vikings ate two meals a day – breakfast and dinner. They ate from wooden bowls with spoons and knives, although they had no forks. The Viking diet consisted of bread with meats such as beef, mutton, seal and elk. They also ate fish, fruit, vegetables and home-made butter and cheese. There was milk, beer or mead (a strong honey wine) to drink. Meat was dried, salted or pickled to preserve it for the winter months.

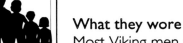

What they wore
Most Viking men wore trousers which reached to the ankle and long-sleeved shirts, or jerkins. The women wore long, loose-fitting dresses which were covered by two rectangular pieces of cloth, and secured at the shoulders by two brooches. The Viking clothing that has survived was mostly made of wool, but skins and furs were also used and traces of linen have even been found.

Part of the family
Viking children did not go to school. Boys went to work with their fathers in the fields. They could go on raids when they were about 16 years old. Girls had to do household tasks, such as weaving and cooking, and help their mothers. Family ties were very strong. Many long and bloody feuds were the result of members of families being insulted by outsiders.

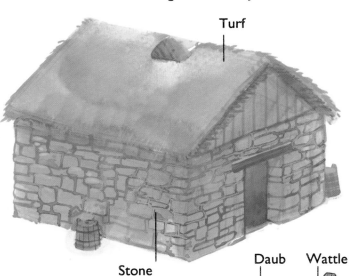

Turf

Stone

Daub   Wattle

Building materials
The Vikings built their houses out of wood or stone, with thatched roofs of straw or reeds. Turf was also used. Some houses had wattle and daub walls. The wattle was made from sticks woven together into a strong framework. This was coated in a daub of mud, straw and animal dung to make it waterproof.

Natural dyes
Viking women often dyed their cloth with natural vegetable dyes. Try making your own vegetable dyes from blackberries or red onion skins. Place the vegetable in a pan and boil it for about three hours (ask an adult to help you). Let the liquid cool and then submerge your material in it. Add some salt to fix the colour, leave the material until you like the colour and then rinse it in cold water.

Nature as evidence
Rubbish pits excavated at the Jorvik site in York, England, have yielded traces of animal, bird and fish bones, nutshells, eggshells and burnt pieces of grain. These give clues to the Viking diet. Many wooden bowls and cups have also survived, preserved by the water-logged peat in which they were buried. Soil samples also reveal what types of plant grew, what kinds of insects there were, and even which parasites lived inside the stomachs of the Jorvik citizens.

An enlarged view of an insect's body from Jorvik

SERPENTS OF THE SEA

The Vikings are famous for their shipbuilding skills and for their longships which carried them far and wide. Their ships were among the finest built in Europe. There were various kinds of ship, each developed for different uses. One of the best known was the longship, a canoe-shaped warship. Longships were tough enough to withstand the stormiest seas, shallow enough to sail up rivers and yet light enough to be carried overland. They were about 20-30 metres long. Each had a woollen sail, which was often striped red and white or blue and white. The ships could also be rowed when the wind dropped.

Evolution of boats
The Viking ships were the product of a long process of development and refinement. The earliest evidence of Scandinavian ships comes from the Bronze Age. Rock carvings at Kalnes in Norway depict ships with pronged prows and sterns. They were made from wooden frames and, it is thought, covered with ox hides. These early vessels were the forerunners of the plank-built boats of the Iron Age. The long, narrow shape of the Viking longships first appeared in the Nydam ship of the AD 400s, and the strong keel used in the Viking ships was introduced in the Kvalsund Boat in the AD 700s.

Boat building
Viking longships were "clinker-built". This means that they were built from overlapping planks of oak, nailed together. Pine was used for the masts. The joints were stuffed with ropes, moss or animal hair to make them both watertight and flexible in stormy seas.

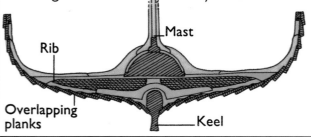

Rib — Mast

Overlapping planks — Keel

Each oarsman packed his belongings into a chest which he then used as a seat while he was rowing.

Steering oar

A solid oak keel formed the backbone of the ship. The keel supported a sturdy mast and a single full sail to propel it forward at great speed when it was windy. Oars could be used in calmer weather.

Natural navigation

With no instruments or maps to guide them, the Vikings depended on sightings of the stars and the Sun to determine direction. They also relied on landmarks and the presence of seaweed or seagulls. By the AD 900s, the Vikings had developed a way of working out the latitude (how far north) in which they were sailing. They used a table of figures, in which the Sun's midday height for each week was recorded, and a measuring stick.

Polar star   **Seaweed**

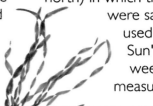

Sea-bird

Viking longships were often called "Serpents of the Sea" because they had figure-heads at the front carved in the shape of fierce dragon or snake heads. The rest of the ship looked like the body of the sea serpent.

RAIDERS AND INVADERS

Driven by the shortage of land at home, the Vikings began their infamous raids in about AD 800. Most raids were carried out by small parties of up to ten boats, each with about 30 warriors on board. The speed and agility of their boats enabled them to make surprise attacks and fast getaways. At first they raided rich churches and monasteries for loot. Later they turned their attention to towns and even began to settle in the places they invaded. The Vikings were brutal but brave warriors. Wherever they went, they spread terror and panic.

The most feared Viking warriors were the berserkers. These warriors may have been drugged to make them lose control of themselves. The word "berserk" is used today to describe a person who behaves wildly.

A Viking raid
The Viking raiders were famed and feared throughout Europe, and many of their exploits were recorded in sagas (see pages 22-23). Imagine you are a Viking, setting off on your first raid across the stormy seas to either France or England. How many ships are in your party? What kind of armour are you wearing? How do you plan to surprise your enemy so that they have no time to defend themselves? And how does your experience compare to the bloody battles and looting of the Vikings detailed in the other sagas?

A Viking helmet

You can make your own Viking helmet out of papier mâché (1). Mould at least three layers of papier mâché around an inflated balloon (2). Allow the papier mâché to dry and burst the balloon. Trim the edges of the papier mâché shell (3) and decorate it (4).

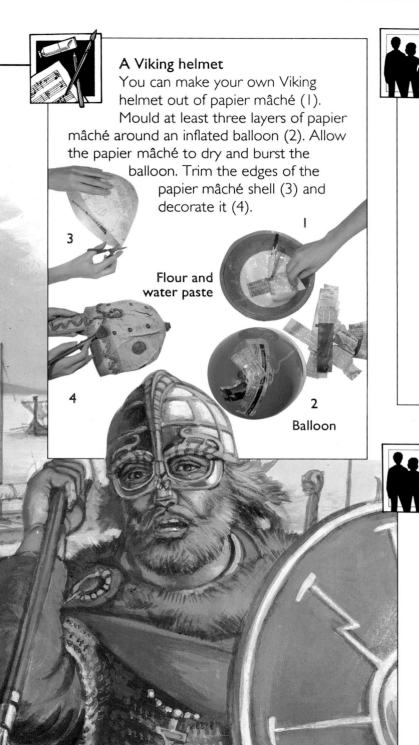

3

Flour and water paste

4

2

Balloon

Women and children

The Vikings looted and plundered the towns they raided and burned most of them to the ground. They showed no mercy to the terrified women or children of the town. Many were murdered along with the men. The women were often tortured before they died. Some were taken prisoner and used or sold as slaves.

Armour and weapons

The Vikings had some of the best armour and weapons in Europe. Ordinary warriors wore tough leather tunics, while the wealthier ones wore armour made from chain mail. All Vikings carried a large round shield, which was sometimes covered with leather. They fought mainly with axes, bows, spears and swords. The Viking sword had a wide, double-edged blade made from iron and steel, and was a warrior's most prized possession.

EXPLORERS AND TRADERS

The Vikings were not simply merciless pirates and raiders. They were also great explorers and traders. The Norwegian Vikings explored and settled in Iceland, Greenland and North America (Vinland). The Danes settled in England, and the Swedes travelled eastwards down the Dnieper River in Russia to the Black Sea and Constantinople. Merchants traded furs, walrus ivory and farm produce for silk, silver and weapons. Thousands of coins, many from Byzantium and the Arab world, have been found in Scandinavia. By the 10th century AD, the Vikings had established a vast network of settlements and trading centres in Europe and beyond.

Knorrs

The Vikings used the knorr mainly for trading purposes. The knorr was a deeper, broader type of boat than the longboat. It was usually equipped with a few oars for navigating harbours or shallow inland waterways. Knorrs could carry a large amount of cargo and a few animals, which were usually kept in the middle of the boat.

The map below shows the Viking settlements and trade, with sailing routes marked by a solid black line. Their influence reached as far east as Constantinople (Istanbul) and as far west as North America. The key below shows the goods traded.

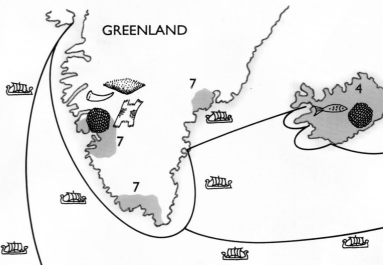

GREENLAND

VINLAND

ATLANTIC OCEAN

Ivory
Furs
Wines
Silks
Fruit
Silver
Weapons
Woollens
Wheat
Timber

Hides
Salt
Jewellery
Spices
Honey
Cloth
Fish
Tin
Slaves

1. AD 700-800
Settlements in the Faroes, Orkneys, Shetlands and Hebrides.
2. AD 820-900
Russian settlements.
3. AD 840-870
Settlements in Ireland.
4. AD 870-930
Settlements in Iceland.
5. AD 876-900
Danelaw established in England.
6. AD 911-940
Settlements in Normandy.
7. AD 980-1000
Settlements in Greenland.
8. AD 1060-1090
Settlements in Sicily.

Distances travelled

Although we cannot be sure of the exact routes taken by the Vikings, the evidence of their settlements does show that they travelled great distances. For example, the journey made by Erik the Red from Iceland to Greenland was over 320 km. If they travelled 20 km a day, how long would their journey have taken them? Using an atlas, plot some of the other routes travelled. How long would it have taken the Vikings to reach these destinations?

False claims

Both Canada and the US have claimed that the Vinland settlement was in their territory. The maple leaf, mentioned in the sagas, was adopted as the Canadian national emblem. Other discoveries in America indicated Viking presence there, but proved to be false. However, evidence discovered in 1962 at L'Anse aux-Meadows in Newfoundland, Canada, verifies the Canadians' claims.

-------Pick up your boat and walk-----

The Vikings owed much of their success in trade to the design of their boats. The Swedes were able to sail far inland up the Russian rivers. When the rivers became too shallow or the traders needed to go overland, they simply picked up their boats and carried them. In this way, they were able to trade with merchants from as far afield as China and Persia.

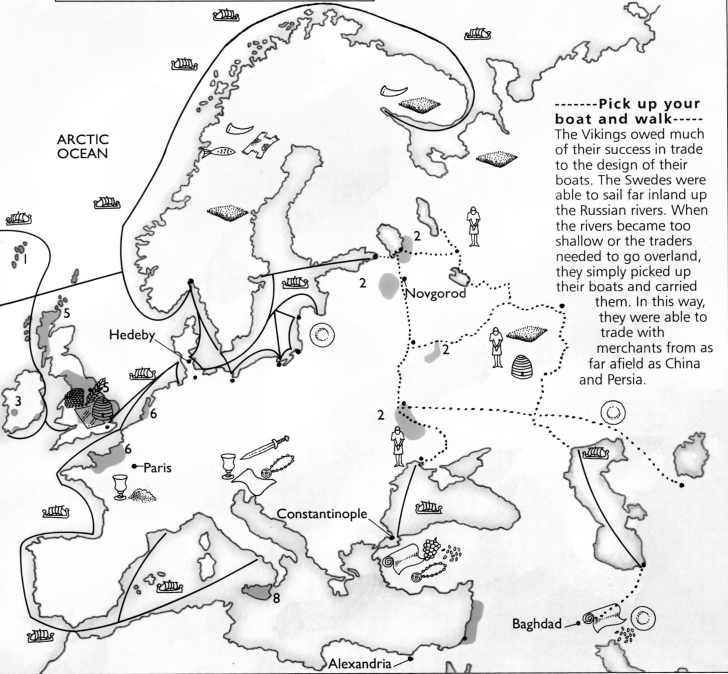

ARCTIC OCEAN

1

5

Hedeby

3

6

6

Paris

Novgorod

2

2

2

2

Constantinople

8

Baghdad

Alexandria

HEDEBY

Hedeby in Viking Denmark was one of the biggest and most important towns in the Viking world. It was a flourishing market town, enjoying a key position on the major trade routes. Merchants came from as far away as France, Russia, Spain and the Middle East to sell their goods. Food and weapons were traded, as well as luxuries such as furs and spices. Craftsmen from the area sold their jewellery, carvings and cloth. Hedeby also had an important slave market, where prisoners of war were sold to the highest bidder. The remains of Hedeby lie about 3 kilometres to the south of the town of Schleswig, in what is now Germany.

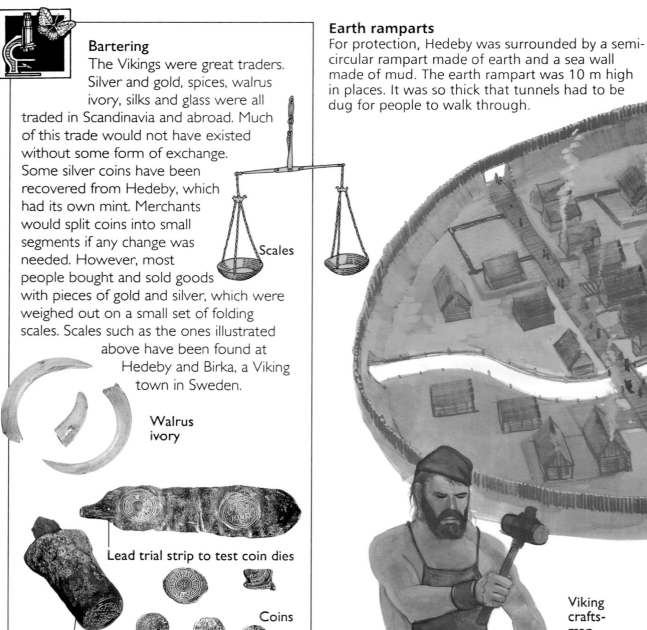

Bartering

The Vikings were great traders. Silver and gold, spices, walrus ivory, silks and glass were all traded in Scandinavia and abroad. Much of this trade would not have existed without some form of exchange. Some silver coins have been recovered from Hedeby, which had its own mint. Merchants would split coins into small segments if any change was needed. However, most people bought and sold goods with pieces of gold and silver, which were weighed out on a small set of folding scales. Scales such as the ones illustrated above have been found at Hedeby and Birka, a Viking town in Sweden.

Scales

Walrus ivory

Lead trial strip to test coin dies

Coin die

Coins

Earth ramparts

For protection, Hedeby was surrounded by a semi-circular rampart made of earth and a sea wall made of mud. The earth rampart was 10 m high in places. It was so thick that tunnels had to be dug for people to walk through.

Viking crafts-man

Archaeological evidence

In about AD 1050, Hedeby was raided and burned to the ground by King Harald Hardradi of Norway. It never really recovered. Today, only the massive earth rampart can still be seen. Archaeologists began to excavate the site in the 1930s. Among many thousands of items, they have found the remains of wooden houses and wells. The timber had been very well preserved in the waterlogged soil. One of the largest trading centres in Britain was at Jorvik (York), shown right. Archaeologists have reconstructed a Viking street from rows of shops and workhouses uncovered there.

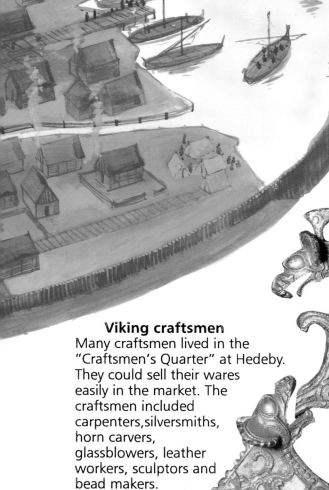

Viking craftsmen

Many craftsmen lived in the "Craftsmen's Quarter" at Hedeby. They could sell their wares easily in the market. The craftsmen included carpenters, silversmiths, horn carvers, glassblowers, leather workers, sculptors and bead makers.

Jewellery

The Vikings enjoyed wearing all kinds of jewellery, including silver brooches, bracelets, necklaces and rings. Try making a piece of Viking jewellery from modelling clay. Plait together three long strands of different coloured clay. Mould four balls of clay into dragon or serpent heads for the ends. Try experimenting with different designs.

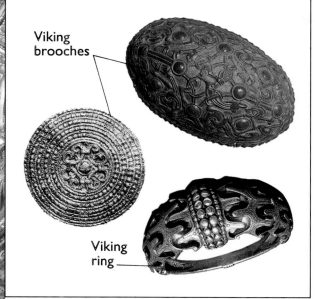

Viking brooches

Viking ring

LAW AND ORDER

The Vikings had no central government, legal system or police force. Each of the many communities had its own council, called the Thing. This was made up of the nobles and freemen of the area. They met regularly to settle arguments, listen to grievances, elect kings and judge criminals. Fines were a common form of punishment. One type of fine, called a wergeld, was paid by a murderer to his victim's family. The amount of the fine represented the monetary value of the dead man. Fines had to be paid in public. Some criminals were banished. Others had to perform tasks to prove their innocence. This was called trial by ordeal.

The Icelandic Althing

Iceland had its own national council, called the Althing. It first met in AD 930 and then met every midsummmer. At first it consisted of 39 chieftains, presided over by an elected Lawspeaker. The Althing lasted for two weeks and was a great social event. The Icelandic parliament today is still called the Althing. The parliament of the Isle of Man meets every summer on the site of the island's Viking Thing.

Isle of Man flag

Thingvellir, the site of the Althing, is a huge plain at the north end of Lake Olfusvatn in Iceland. The lava cliff was called the Logberg, or Law Rock. This was the platform for the speakers. The flag in the picture below marks the site of the Althing.

The *Havamal*

In addition to the laws agreed at the Thing, the Vikings also had a series of sayings relating to everyday life. The *Havamal* was compiled in the 9th century and was a kind of survival handbook, offering advice such as: *Be a friend to your friend, match gift with gift; meet smiles with smiles, and lies with dissimulation. Look carefully round doorways before you walk in; you never know when an enemy might be there.*

Women's rights

Viking women had more rights than the women of other European societies at the time. They were allowed to own land and other property, and a wife had the right to a share in the wealth earned by her husband. Women could also act as farmers and traders and get divorced. They were expected to defend the homestead when their men were away a-Viking.

The *Jonsbok*

At first Viking laws were not written down, but passed from one generation to the next by word of mouth. The ancient code of Icelandic laws can be found inscribed on vellum (see page 23) in the *Jonsbok*. The illumination (illustration) shown opposite comes from a 16th century vellum copy of the *Jonsbok*. A 14th century copy of the *Jonsbok* can also be found in the Royal Library, Copenhagen, Denmark.

The Holmganga duel

The Holmganga duel had very strict rules. It was fought on a piece of cloth 3 sq m. If either man stepped off the cloth, he was considered a coward.

At the end of the duel, the man with the most sword wounds had to pay his opponent in silver. If he died, the victor won his property. Duels were usually to the death.

VIKING BURIALS

When a Viking died, he or she might be buried or cremated, in a ship or in the ground. This depended on the individual's position in society and on their wealth. Viking funerals were times of great ceremony. The Vikings believed in life after death, so dead people were buried with some of their personal possessions to ease their journey into the next world. Huge Viking cemeteries and burial mounds have been found at towns such as Jelling in Denmark. Some of the graves were marked by stones placed in the shape of ships.

A middle-class burial

Middle-class Vikings were buried in wooden chambers, with food and drink for their journey and other personal belongings. Items such as combs and spindles have also been found in Viking graves. Warriors were buried in full battle dress, with their swords and shields.

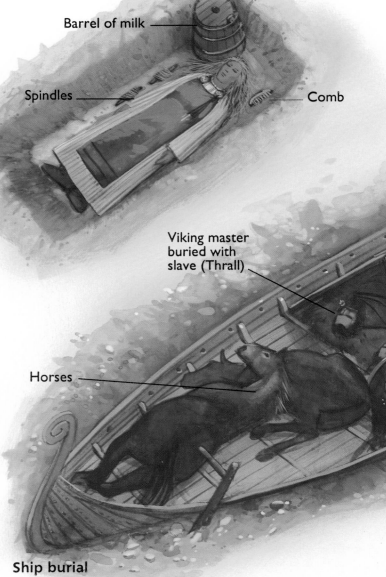

Barrel of milk

Spindles

Comb

Viking master buried with slave (Thrall)

Horses

Site evidence

Most of the evidence about the Vikings and their ships comes from the grave mounds. Ships were used for the burial of wealthy people only. Although the tradition was carried out before the Viking Age, it was also very popular among the Vikings. Two of the finest Viking ships, from Gokstad and Oseberg (see pages 26-27), were uncovered as ship burials. If the burial site was far from the sea, or if the family could not afford a ship, stones in the shape of a ship were placed around the burial site.

Ship burial

Kings, queens and great chieftains were sometimes buried in ships which were then buried under huge mounds or burnt. The mourners believed that the ship would carry the dead person safely to the next world. Their belongings were buried or burnt with them, including their horses, dogs and even slaves.

Modern day festivals

Every year, on the last Tuesday of January, the people of Lerwick in Shetland relive their Viking history. They celebrate Up-Helly-Aa, a modern version of a Viking fire festival. A model of a Viking longboat is pulled through the town by a torchlit procession which includes a "jarl" and his band of Viking warriors. Many of the participants actually dress up as Vikings. The ship is set alight to represent the funeral pyre of a Viking chieftain. This is followed by all-night feasting and singing.

During Up-Helly-Aa, the Viking galley burns furiously as the festival reaches its climax.

Hunting dog and dead man's possessions

The funeral pyre
The Vikings had great faith in the power of fire. They believed that if a warrior's body was burnt on a funeral pyre, his spirit would go to Valhalla, the Viking warriors' destination in Asgard (see page 20).

Broken shield

Bent sword

Spear

Sacrifices

One of the most fascinating accounts of the sacrifices and rituals that accompanied Viking burials comes from an Arab trader called Ibn Fadlan. He described the ship cremation of a rich and important Viking chieftain. A young slave woman from the chieftain's household was chosen to die with her master. A ship was drawn up onto the land and surrounded with firewood. It was then filled with the chieftain's most prized possessions and his body was placed on a couch. The young servant girl lay at her master's side and was sacrificed by an old woman called the Angel of Death. She was "a stout and grim figure" who was in charge of such rituals. A relative of the dead man then stepped from the crowd, naked, and set the boat ablaze with a torch.

Angel of Death

19

GODS AND RELIGION

Until their conversion to Christianity in the 10th and 11th centuries, the Vikings worshipped many gods. The most important were Odin, Thor and Frey. Odin was the chief god and the god of battle. He ruled Asgard, the home of the gods. Thor was the god of thunder and lightning. He rode across the sky in a mighty chariot, with which he made the noise of thunder, wielding his huge hammer, Mjollnir. Many Vikings wore Mjollnir pendants as a protection against evil. Frey was the son of Njord (see below) and was associated with farming and fertility.

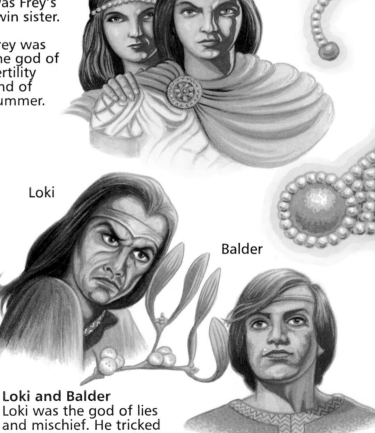

Njord was the god of the sea and the father of the twins, Frey and Freya.

Freya was a fertility goddess and also goddess of beauty, love, war and death. She was Frey's twin sister.

Frey was the god of fertility and of summer.

Loki

Balder

Loki and Balder
Loki was the god of lies and mischief. He tricked the god Hoder into killing his brother, Balder. Loki was jealous of Balder's beauty and popularity.

Days of the week
Some days of the week are named after Viking gods. Tyr's day (Tuesday) is named after Tyr, god of war. Woden's day (Wednesday) comes from Woden, or Odin. Thor's day (Thursday) is from Thor and Frigga's day (Friday) from Frigga, wife of Odin.

VALHALLA
Valhalla was the hall in Asgard to which the Viking warriors slain in battle were sent. They were called the Einheriar. The Einheriar were led to Asgard by the Valkyries, beautiful young women sent by Odin. Each day in Asgard, the Einheriar would do battle, inflicting and suffering mortal wounds. Each night they were brought back to life and healed of any injuries. Then they returned to Valhalla to enjoy a great feast.

Asgard

Asgard, the home of the gods, was invisible to human eyes because it floated above the Earth. It was separated from Earth by a river, called Ifing.

Odin, the chief god

Thor, the god of thunder

Ragnarok

Viking mythology was concerned with life after death and about what would happen in the distant future, when all the gods were killed. Ragnarok was to be the final battle between the forces of good and evil, between the gods and the giants and monsters. Odin, Thor and Frey, amongst others, would die. However, some of the gods would survive and build a new and better world.

Types of worship

In AD 950, another Arab traveller called Ibrahim al-Tartushi visited Hedeby. In his account of his travels, he describes the rituals followed by citizens who had made sacrifices to the gods. The bodies of sacrificed animals — either an ox, a ram, a goat or a pig — were put onto poles outside the door of his house. In this way, his neighbours learned of his pious deed.

LANGUAGE & LITERATURE

The Vikings were great poets and storytellers. Court poets, called skalds, praised the brave deeds of kings in their verses. There were also tales of great heroes, warriors and battles. These were called the sagas. Sagas were passed on by word of mouth, until they were written down by scholars in the 13th century. The Viking alphabet consisted of letters, called runes. Each rune was made up of straight lines so it could be carved into wood or stone with a chisel or knife. The sagas, however, were written down in Latin, not in runes.

The scene shown right is one of several carved into the wood of Hylestad church in Norway. The scenes depict Sigurd, a Viking hero, testing the blade of his sword. The blade snaps and Regin, the blacksmith, has to forge another one. Sigurd later uses the new blade to kill a dragon who is guarding some treasure.

A	B	C	D	E	F	G	H	I	K	L	M

A secret code
The runic alphabet, or *futhark*, was invented about 2,000 years ago.
Runes were traditionally associated with magic and mystery, and were often used as a kind of secret code for charms or curses. Write your own secret message using the Runic alphabet shown above. Can you work out what we've written here?

Writing it down

The Viking sagas were first written down in the 13th century on calfskin (vellum). Sharpened quill feathers from swans or ravens were used as pens, and a glossy ink was distilled from berries.

An extract from the *Flateyjarbok*. This illumination depicts the death of St Olaf at Strikesland.

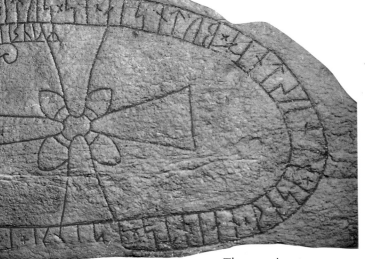

The runic stone above can be found by a roadside in Sweden. It commemorates a Viking farmer who visited Jerusalem and died in Greece.

Runes in literature

Many writers of fantasy or science fiction books have invented languages based on runes. In "The Hobbit", the author, J R R Tolkien, uses magical runes as the alphabet of the dwarves. They used it to mark secret doors, write secret instructions and keep secret records.

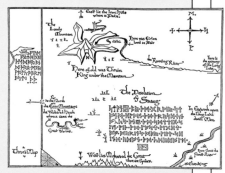

| N | O | P | Q | R | S | T | U | V | W | X | Y | Z |

Naming places

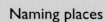

Lots of everyday words come from the Vikings, such as freckle, leg and law. As the Vikings settled in their new lands, they often gave the places where they lived Viking names. Many of these names survive today. For example, Milford in Wales comes from the Viking words "melr" (meaning sandbank) and fjord (meaning valley). Other Viking names include the words dale (valley), kirk (church) and beck (brook or stream). The town of Schleswig in Germany (see page 14) comes from the term "vik-place", which means a place where the Vikings went raiding or trading. Surnames can also be seen to reflect Viking influences. Nott, for example, comes from the great Viking chief, Canute.

THE DANES

The Vikings can be roughly divided into three groups according to where they came from, although they often overlapped. On their raids, the Danes mainly went to England, France, Germany and Spain. They invaded England in AD 865 and ruled in the east of the country. This area became known as the Danelaw. They were prevented from spreading westwards by King Alfred the Great of Wessex. In France, the Danes struck a deal with the king, Charles II. In AD 886, their chief, Rollo, gained control of Normandy, in France.

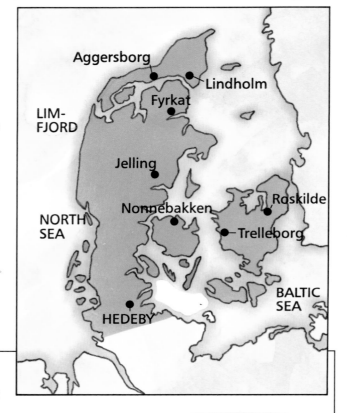

This map shows Denmark at the time of the Vikings. Denmark today (see photo, left) consists of the Jutland peninsula, two large islands and almost 500 smaller islands. In Viking times it included part of southern Sweden. In the south, the Viking frontier was defended by the Danevirke, a huge earth rampart. In the north, the Limfjord provided a vital sailing route through northern Jutland.

Lindholm Høje

Lindholm Høje is one of the greatest Viking burial grounds to be found in Scandinavia. The majority of graves contained cremations dating from AD 500 onwards. Around AD 800, the stone settings around the graves became ship-shaped, illustrating the Viking belief in the ship as a symbol of the journey into the afterworld. A town was also discovered near the cemetery. Here, one of the most famous artefacts of the Viking age was found – the Urnes Brooch. Many replicas of Viking jewellery depict the graceful animal motif on the brooch.

The ornamental Urnes style of the Viking period takes its name from the Norwegian stave-church at Urnes. Part of the elaborately carved north portal is shown here.

Feasts and festivals

All Vikings loved festivals, and huge feasts were held for Viking men returning home from a raid. At these feasts, families were reunited, gossip was exchanged, and weddings were arranged. There were three major feasts a year. The first took place at the beginning of the year, the second in April, and the third at the end of October to celebrate the harvest. Feasts were usually accompanied by entertainment in the form of poetry recitals and music.

The Jelling stone

The Jelling stone was set up at Jelling in Denmark in the AD 980s by King Harald Bluetooth, as a memorial to his parents who were buried there. One side of the stone shows a crucifixion, another bears a runic inscription, and the third (above) depicts an imaginary animal with a snake wrapped around its body.

Games

Dice games and pegboard games were popular among all the Vikings, as were games such as draughts and chess. In the evenings, Viking children would sit around the hearth and amuse themselves by making up short poems, like limericks, stories and riddles.

A Viking chessboard

Kings of Denmark

For much of the Viking Age, Denmark did not have one overall king. For a time, it was ruled by kings from Sweden. Then, in the AD 930s or 940s, Gorm the Old became king and united Denmark. He was succeeded by his son, Harald Bluetooth, who ruled until 986. Harald was overthrown by his son, Swein Forkbeard. Forkbeard's son, Canute, ruled over Denmark, Norway and England from 1014-1035.

King Harald Bluetooth was baptised a Christian after seeing a Christian missionary pick up a red-hot metal bar.

Kingy bats was played with a bat and a ball.

THE NORWEGIANS

The Norwegians began their raids with the attack on Lindisfarne in AD 793 (see page 5). They also struck many other places in Europe. Then their attention turned westwards to the North Atlantic. In the late 800s the first group of Vikings went to Iceland. By the late 980s there were also Norwegian settlers in Greenland. Then, in about 1000, Leif Erikson, son of Erik the Red, led a party even further west to North America. They landed in Newfoundland, Canada, which they called Vinland because so many wine-making grapes grew there.

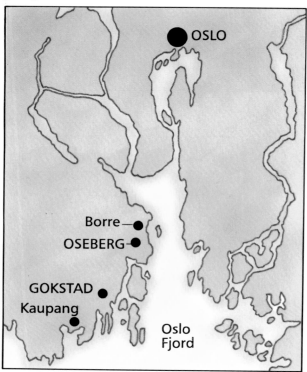

The Gokstad and Oseberg ships

In 1893, a reconstruction of a 9th century Viking ship found at Gokstad sailed across the Atlantic Ocean from Norway to Newfoundland, Canada. This proved that the Vikings could have reached North America long before Columbus. Another famous ship find, the 9th century Oseberg burial ship, was found in 1904. It contained the skeletons of a queen and her servant. Buried with her were kitchen equipment, sledges, horses, two oxen for food, animal-head posts and a richly-carved wagon. There were also fragments of tapestries. Both ships are now on display at a museum near Oslo, Norway.

A lion-headed post from furniture in the Oseberg ship (above). Burial wagon (below).

Erik the Red and Greenland

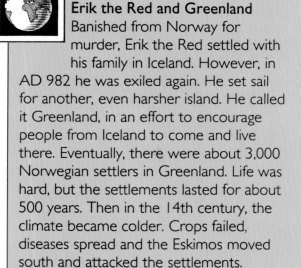

Banished from Norway for murder, Erik the Red settled with his family in Iceland. However, in AD 982 he was exiled again. He set sail for another, even harsher island. He called it Greenland, in an effort to encourage people from Iceland to come and live there. Eventually, there were about 3,000 Norwegian settlers in Greenland. Life was hard, but the settlements lasted for about 500 years. Then in the 14th century, the climate became colder. Crops failed, diseases spread and the Eskimos moved south and attacked the settlements.

Competitions

Games that prepared the participants for battle were extremely popular among the Vikings. Many sagas describe wrestling matches to find the strongest wrestler. Swimming competitions were also popular, as were fencing, boulder-throwing and archery. The Viking's favourite pastime was horse-fighting, for which stallions were specially bred.

Stallion fighting

A detail from the cradle of the wagon shown below

The beautifully carved prow from the Oseberg ship

Kings of Norway

The Norwegian Royal family was descended from Harald Fine Hair. Hakon I claimed the throne in AD 935. He was killed in battle in AD 960. His successor was Olaf Tryggvason, who was killed at the Battle of Svolder in AD 1000. The Danish king, Swein Forkbeard then came to power. When he died, his son, Canute, and St Olaf (II), became rivals for the Norwegian throne. Canute defeated St Olaf at the Battle of Stiklestad in AD 1030 and became king of Norway. Later kings were Magnus, Harald Hardrada, Magnus II and Olaf III.

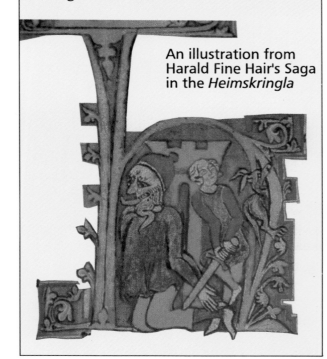

An illustration from Harald Fine Hair's Saga in the *Heimskringla*

THE SWEDES

The Swedish Vikings turned their attention eastwards. In the early AD 800s, they began to send raiding parties along the rivers into Russia, where they eventually set up a vast network of trading posts. They were called "Rus" by the Slavic people of the area. Some Swedes followed the rivers to the Black Sea and to the wealthy city of Constantinople, which is now called Istanbul. Others sailed down to the Caspian Sea and traded with merchants from Persia. The Swedes were converted to Christianity in the early 11th century, under the rule of King Olaf Skottkönung.

Uppsala

Uppsala in Sweden was the site of one of the most notorious pagan cult centres in Scandinavia. The details of a festival which was held there every nine years were recorded by a German cleric called Adam of Bremen in AD 1075. He wrote of sacrifices being carried out in a sacred grove which stood next to a pagan temple. Nine heads of each kind of male creature, both human and animal, were offered to the gods. There was also a large tree near the grove. At the roots of the tree was a well where human sacrifices were made. If the body of the victim sank without trace, it meant the sacrifice had been accepted by the gods.

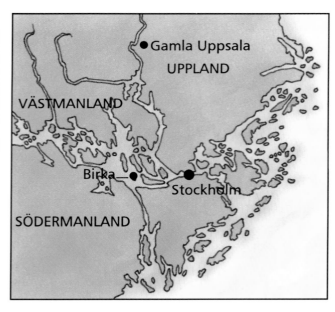

The map above shows Sweden during the Viking Age. Like the other Vikings, the Swedes had little suitable land for their growing population. Their raids were both for trading and for setting up colonies.

Winter activites

During the long months of the harsh Scandinavian winter, many Viking men occupied themselves with repairing their tools and forging new weapons. There was also skating, skiing and sledging, and, of course, snowball fights. Viking skates uncovered at Jorvik were made from animal bones. One side of the bone was polished flat for sliding over the ice, while the other side was made into a point.

The skates were attached to shoes with leather ties. Long poles were used to push the skater over the snow.

Gotland

Gotland is an island in the Baltic Sea, off the east coast of Sweden. It claimed to be the centre of the Viking world. It was indeed at the centre of the Viking trade routes and became wealthy and thriving as a result. Thousands of Viking artefacts have been found at Gotland. They include nearly 400 carved picture stones. The picture stone below shows ships and warriors being welcomed to Valhalla.

Russia and beyond

The Viking's chief interest in the East was trade. The Swedish Vikings travelled down the Volkhov and Dnieper Rivers to Russia. In the AD 860s, three Scandinavian brothers were asked by the Slavs "to restore order and to rule over them". The land the brothers ruled was known as "the land of the Rus", from which "Russia" comes. Swedish Vikings also travelled east to Byzantium, where they were bodyguards to the Byzantine Emperor. They were known as the Varangian Guard.

One of the oldest crucifixes found in Scandinavia

The decline of the Vikings

In 1066, at the Battle of Stamford Bridge, the Norwegian king, Harald Hardradi, was killed trying to conquer the English. Hedeby was also destroyed that year by Polish tribesmen. Many of the Viking raiders began to settle in their chosen lands. Vinland was abandoned and forgotten until Columbus's voyage there in 1492. In Europe, feudal systems of government were introduced, with well trained and equipped armies. The Vikings were no match for these soldiers, and the terrifying raids and invasions which had characterised the Viking Age ceased.

The Bayeux Tapestry (right) records the Norman invasion of England by William the Conqueror, a Norman descendant of the Viking chief, Rollo (see page 24).

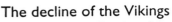

AD 789 Viking ships off southern England

793 Lindisfarne, Iona and Jarrow raided

795 Viking raid near Dublin

835 Beginning of 30 years of raiding on England, Germany and France

843 Rus attack Byzantium (Istanbul)

around 860 Iceland discovered. National monarchies established in Norway, Sweden and Denmark. Halvdan united Norway (850) and Gorm united DenmarK (860)

862 Vikings begin trading in Russia

866 Danish kingdom established at York

872-930 Norwegians settle in the Orkneys and Shetlands

875-900 Colonization of Iceland

866 Vikings control the English Danelaw

911 Vikings granted control of Normandy

934 Germans capture Hedeby

around 965 Harald Bluetooth of Denmark becomes a Christian, as does Hakon the Good of Norway

986 Erik the Red settles Greenland

985-986 Viking explorers sight America (Vinland)

around 1000 Norway, Greenland and Iceland become Christian

1017-35 Reign of Canute the Great

1066 English defeat Norwegians at Stamford Bridge; Normans defeat English at Hastings

8000BC

First hieroglyphs (picture writing) in Egypt c.3500BC

Old Kingdom in Egypt 2628-2181 BC.

Pyramids built in Egypt during Old Kingdom

Egyptian Middle Kingdom 2181-1567 BC

2000BC

Tutankhamun - the boy pharaoh

New Kingdom in Egypt 1567-1085 BC

Romulus and Remus found the city of Rome 753 BC

500BC

Roman Empire c.27 BC-c.AD 476

Julius Caesar murdered 44 BC

Fall of the Roman Empire AD 476

Viking raids on Britain and France AD 793-1000

AD1000

First Crusade to recapture Holy Land from Muslims AD1096

First mechanical clock developed

The Aztec Empire in Central America AD 1300-1521

AD 1350-1532 Growth of the Inca Empire in South America

8000-5650 BC
First cities – Jericho and Catal Hüyük

3500-3000 BC
Wheel invented by the Sumerians

2500-1500 BC
Rise of the Indus Valley civilization

Early Minoan period in Crete begins c.2500 BC

Stonehenge completed in England c.1500 BC

The destruction of Knossos in Crete. End of the Minoan period c.1200 BC

c.500 BC Life of Gautama the Buddha

c.1400-1027 BC Shang dynasty in China.

Birth of Confucius 551 BC

The Golden Age of Greece 478-405 BC

Alexander the Great conquers Persia, Syria and Eygpt 331 BC

The first Empire in China 221 BC-AD 618

The Great Wall in China completed in 214 BC.

Samurai warriors of Japan from AD 1100-1850

The Plague, or Black Death, spread throughout Europe AD 1347.

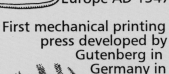

First mechanical printing press developed by Gutenberg in Germany in AD 1455.

Christopher Columbus sets sail for the West Indies and became the first European to discover America.

GLOSSARY

Althing The national council of Iceland.

Asgard The home of the Viking gods.

Berserker The most feared Viking warrior who fought wildly in battles.

Danelaw The area of eastern England which was ruled by the Danish Vikings.

Einheriar The name given to Viking warriors killed in battle. This was the most honourable way to die and meant that the warriors would enjoy a glorious afterlife in Valhalla.

Jarls Rich noblemen in Viking society. Members of the Viking upper class and powerful landowners. The English word "earl" comes from the Viking jarl.

Karls Freemen in Viking society who included farmers, merchants and craftsmen. They were below jarls in the Viking social order.

Ragnarok The final battle between the Viking gods (the forces of good) and the giants and monsters (the forces of evil).

Runes The characters, or symbols, which made up the Viking alphabet.

Rus The name given to the Swedish Vikings who travelled eastwards to trade in what is now called Russia.

Saga A story about Viking battles, warrior heroes or gods.

Skalds Court poets who celebrated the deeds of the Viking kings in verse.

Thing The council which governed a Viking community. The Thing met to settle arguments and judge criminals.

Thralls Thralls were slaves, the lowest rank in Viking society. They had very few rights. Many slaves were prisoners of war.

Valhalla A hall in Asgard where Viking warriors slain in battle were thought to go to when they died.

INDEX

Photographic credits

All pictures were supplied by CM Dixon Photo Resources apart from cover right, 9, 11 top all, 12 top, 14 top & 20 top: Roger Vlitos; 4 & 5: Spectrum 6-7 all, 8, 15 top & middle right, 18 top, 19, 22 top, 24 top, 25 middle & 28 bottom: York Archaeological Trust; 16 all, 24 middle & 26 top: Frank Spooner Pictures; 17: Institute of Copenhagen; 20 bottom, 21 & 29 bottom: Mary Evans; 23 top & 27 bottom right: by kind permission of the Manuscript Institute of Iceland; 23 bottom: illustrated by JRR Tolkien with permission of Grafton Books, an imprint of HarperCollins Publisher Ltd; 26 middle & bottom & 27 top: University of Oslo.

PRINTED IN BELGIUM BY
proost
INTERNATIONAL BOOK PRODUCTION